The Phoenix Blueprint

Meena Rohith Vignesh

Published by Meena Rohith Vignesh, 2024.

THE

PHOENIX
BLUEPRINT

COPYRIGHTS

Self published
First Edition

Table of Contents

For my husband, who stood with me in anything and everything, and for making me who I am as a woman today .

DEDICATION

For my one and only husband who stood as my core to everything for improving and making me who I am today

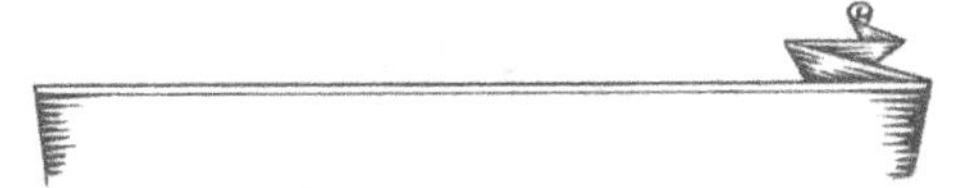

TABLE OF CONTENTS

INTRODUCTIOn

The Phoenix: A Symbol of Transformation and Resilience

Introduction

Throughout history, myths and symbols have served as powerful tools to convey human experiences and emotions.

Among these, the phoenix stands out as a profound representation of transformation and resilience.

Often depicted as a magnificent bird that rises from its own ashes, the phoenix encapsulates the idea of rebirth and renewal after adversity.

This symbolism resonates deeply, particularly in the context of women's empowerment, illustrating how rising from challenges can lead to significant personal growth and strength

The Phoenix as a Symbol of Transformation

THE PHOENIX IS ROOTED in various cultures and mythologies, where it is often associated with fire, rebirth, and the cyclical nature of life. The most recognized narrative tells of the phoenix being consumed by flames, only to emerge renewed and rejuvenated. This imagery powerfully reflects the transformative processes that individuals, particularly women, undergo in their lives.

For many women, the journey toward empowerment is often paved with challenges and societal pressures that seek to confine them to traditional roles.

The phoenix represents the courage to confront these obstacles and transform them into opportunities for growth.

Each phase of struggle—whether it be battling discrimination, overcoming personal loss, or breaking free from societal expectations—serves as a catalyst for transformation.

In this light, the phoenix encourages women to embrace their own journeys of self-discovery. Just as the phoenix rises from ashes, women can redefine their identities and assert their voices, often discovering inner strengths they were previously unaware of. The transformative journey emphasizes that change is not something to fear; rather, it is a crucial part of personal evolution and empowerment.

Resilience in the Face of Adversity

RESILIENCE IS A KEY theme intertwined with the symbolism of the phoenix. The ability to rise from the ashes signifies not just survival, but thriving in the face of adversity. For women, resilience often manifests in their responses to challenges that threaten their aspirations and well-being.

Consider the stories of women like Malala Yousafzai, who, after surviving an assassination attempt for advocating girls' education, transformed her personal trauma into a global movement for change. Her journey exemplifies the phoenix's essence: rising from despair to inspire millions. This narrative illustrates how resilience can propel individuals not only to overcome their circumstances but also to effect positive change in society.

The act of rising from challenges fosters a sense of community and solidarity among women. When one woman's story of resilience is shared, it becomes a beacon of hope for others. The phoenix symbolizes this interconnectedness; when women uplift one another, they collectively rise, creating a powerful network of support. This sense of community amplifies the impact of their individual journeys, reinforcing the idea that resilience is not a solitary endeavor but a shared experience.

Embracing Growth and Empowerment

EMBRACING GROWTH THROUGH challenges is central to the phoenix's narrative and vital for women's empowerment. Each setback can serve as a crucial lesson, providing insights that contribute to personal and communal development.

The phoenix encourages individuals to view failures as opportunities for learning rather than as definitive endpoints.

In the context of women's empowerment, embracing growth means advocating for oneself and others. Women are increasingly recognizing the importance of self-advocacy in various spheres—personal, professional, and social.

The phoenix symbolizes this call to action; by rising from challenges, women assert their rights and influence, challenging societal norms that seek to limit them.

Moreover, fostering environments that encourage personal growth is essential. Workshops, mentorship programs, and supportive networks can help women harness their potential and turn obstacles into stepping stones for success.

By creating spaces where women can share their stories and learn from one another, society can cultivate a culture of resilience and empowerment.

The phoenix also emphasizes the importance of redefining success. Women must understand that their value is not solely tied to traditional achievements but is rooted in their ability to navigate life's challenges. Each moment of struggle, every rise from the ashes, contributes to a rich tapestry of experience that enhances their strength and character.

The phoenix, as a symbol of transformation and resilience, profoundly encapsulates the journey of women toward empowerment.

By rising from the ashes of adversity, women illustrate an incredible capacity for growth, strength, and renewal. The stories of those who embrace their challenges and transform their lives serve as powerful reminders that empowerment is possible, even in the face of significant obstacles.

As society continues to evolve, recognizing and celebrating the resilience of women becomes increasingly vital. The phoenix teaches us that from hardship comes new beginnings, and that every challenge can lead to personal and collective growth. By fostering an environment that encourages transformation and resilience, we empower women to rise—not just for themselves but for future generations, creating a legacy of strength and empowerment that mirrors the enduring spirit of the phoenix.

Setting the Stage for Self-Discovery and Empowerment

Introduction

In an age where external influences often overshadow personal truths, the journey of self-discovery has never been more critical. Setting the stage for self-discovery and empowerment involves creating an environment where individuals can explore their identities, values, and aspirations without fear of judgment. This process not only enhances personal growth but also enables individuals to reclaim their narratives, fostering a deeper understanding of themselves. This essay will discuss the significance of self-discovery, the steps involved in creating a supportive environment, and encourage readers to reflect on their personal journeys toward empowerment.

Self-discovery is the process of exploring one's inner self—values, beliefs, passions, and potential. This journey is crucial because it lays the foundation for empowerment. When individuals understand who they are, they can make informed choices that align with their true selves, rather than conforming to societal expectations or external pressures.

Many individuals, especially women, grapple with societal norms that dictate how they should behave, look, or pursue their ambitions. This disconnect can lead to feelings of inadequacy and self-doubt. By engaging in self-discovery, individuals can confront these pressures, dismantling the barriers that hinder their growth. Self-discovery encourages authenticity, allowing individuals to embrace their uniqueness and cultivate self-confidence.

Furthermore, self-discovery is not a one-time event; it is a continuous journey. Life experiences, challenges, and personal relationships all contribute to this evolving process. By remaining open to self-reflection, individuals can adapt to changes and continuously redefine their paths, fostering resilience and empowerment.

Creating a Supportive Environment

TO EMBARK ON A MEANINGFUL journey of self-discovery, it is essential to create a supportive environment that nurtures introspection and growth. This involves both internal and external factors.

1. Internal Reflection:

Setting aside time for self-reflection is vital. This can be achieved through journaling, meditation, or simply quiet contemplation. These practices allow individuals to connect with their thoughts and emotions, facilitating deeper insights into their desires and motivations. Reflective practices encourage honesty and vulnerability, which are crucial for authentic self-discovery.

1. Seeking Support:

Surrounding oneself with supportive individuals can enhance the self-discovery process. Friends, mentors, or support groups that encourage open dialogue can provide valuable perspectives and insights. These relationships create safe spaces where individuals can share their experiences, fears, and aspirations without judgment. The encouragement and understanding from others can serve as powerful motivators during challenging times.

1. Setting Boundaries:

In a world filled with distractions and pressures, setting healthy boundaries is essential. This might involve limiting exposure to negative influences, whether they stem from social media, toxic relationships, or unrealistic societal expectations. By prioritizing self-care and well-being, individuals can create an environment that fosters personal growth and empowerment.

1.　Embracing Challenges:

The journey of self-discovery often involves confronting discomfort and challenges. Embracing these moments as opportunities for growth can lead to profound insights. Rather than shying away from difficult experiences, individuals should view them as essential parts of their journeys, contributing to their strength and resilience.

Encouraging Reflection on Personal Journeys

ENCOURAGING READERS to reflect on their journeys is a crucial step in fostering self-discovery and empowerment. Each individual's path is unique, and shaped by experiences, values, and dreams. By taking the time to reflect, individuals can identify the milestones that have shaped their identities and aspirations.

1.　Identifying Key Moments:

Reflect on significant experiences that have influenced your life. Consider moments of joy, struggle, and transformation. What lessons did these experiences teach you? How have they shaped your identity? Acknowledging these key moments can help individuals understand their journeys and recognize their strengths.

1.　Recognizing Patterns:

Examine recurring themes or patterns in your life. Are there beliefs or habits that have held you back? Conversely, what strengths have you consistently drawn upon? Understanding these patterns can provide valuable insights into areas for growth and development.

1. Articulating Aspirations:

Take time to articulate your dreams and aspirations. What do you truly desire for yourself? What steps can you take to align your actions with your goals? By clarifying your aspirations, you can set a course for your journey, empowering yourself to pursue your passions unapologetically.

1. Embracing Vulnerability:

Reflecting on your journey requires vulnerability. It's essential to confront both strengths and weaknesses honestly. Embracing vulnerability allows individuals to connect with their authentic selves and fosters a deeper understanding of their needs and desires.

SETTING THE STAGE FOR self-discovery and empowerment is a transformative process that requires intention, reflection, and support. By prioritizing self-exploration, individuals can uncover their true selves, embracing authenticity and resilience. Creating a supportive environment—both internally and externally—fosters personal growth and strengthens the foundation for empowerment.

Encouraging reflection on personal journeys allows individuals to appreciate their unique paths and the lessons learned along the way. By engaging in this process, readers can reclaim their narratives and embark on a journey toward empowerment that is both meaningful and fulfilling. Ultimately, self-discovery is not just about finding oneself; it is about empowering oneself to live authentically and courageously in a world that often demands conformity.

Chapter 1: Understanding Strength

Defining Strength: Beyond Stereotypes

For centuries, strength has often been equated with physical power, an archetype molded by cultural narratives that glorify brute force and unwavering stoicism. Images of muscular heroes, champions of endurance, and unwavering leaders dominate our media, leaving little room for the subtler, yet equally profound forms of strength. These traditional views, while compelling, carry limitations that can distort our understanding of what it means to be truly strong.

As we embark on a journey to redefine strength, it's essential to consider its multifaceted nature. Strength can be emotional, mental, and spiritual, often hidden beneath the surface of a polished exterior. Emotional strength allows us to confront our feelings and navigate the complexities of relationships. Mental strength empowers us to persevere in the face of adversity, to think critically, and to adapt. Spiritual strength guides us through life's uncertainties, providing a sense of purpose and connection.

When we broaden our definition of strength, we open ourselves to a deeper appreciation of resilience. We recognize that the act of asking for help, the willingness to express our feelings, and the courage to confront our fears are all markers of true strength. This expanded view invites us to celebrate not just the triumphant moments but also the quiet, persistent efforts that define our character.

The Power of Vulnerability

Vulnerability, often misperceived as a weakness, is perhaps the most powerful form of strength we can possess. To be vulnerable is to embrace authenticity and honesty, to expose our true selves without the protective armor we often don to navigate the world. This act of showing our true selves can be daunting, yet it is in this exposure that we find our most profound connections and insights.

Consider the story of a woman named Sarah, who spent years battling the internal demons of anxiety and self-doubt. For a long time, she believed that sharing her struggles would tarnish her image of strength. She presented a façade of perfection at work and home, but inside, she felt fragmented. It was only after a turning point—a moment of crisis—that Sarah found the courage to share her truth with close friends. Rather than the judgment she feared, she was met with compassion and understanding. In that moment, vulnerability became her strength, allowing her to connect with others on a deeper level and ultimately leading to healing.

Another inspiring tale comes from Maria, a single mother who faced financial struggles after her divorce. Initially, she hesitated to share her situation with her friends, fearing their pity. But one evening, overwhelmed by the weight of her circumstances, she opened up during a gathering. To her surprise, her vulnerability fostered a sense of solidarity. Several friends shared their own challenges, creating a supportive network. Maria realized that her honesty not only alleviated her burden but also empowered others to embrace their vulnerabilities.

Together, they transformed their struggles into a shared strength, offering each other support and encouragement.

These stories exemplify a profound truth: embracing vulnerability fosters resilience. When we allow ourselves to be seen, we break down barriers, create empathy, and invite others into our lives. It's through this shared humanity that we uncover the strength that lies within us all.

Cultivating Strength Through Vulnerability

EMBRACING VULNERABILITY is not an easy journey. It requires intentional practice and a willingness to step outside our comfort zones. Here are some strategies for cultivating strength through vulnerability:

1. Self-Reflection:

Take time to explore your feelings and thoughts. Journaling can be a powerful tool for understanding your vulnerabilities. Reflect on moments of fear, insecurity, or doubt and consider how they shape your experiences.

1. Seek Support:

Surround yourself with individuals who encourage authenticity. Create safe spaces where vulnerability is welcomed, allowing for open dialogue about struggles and triumphs.

1. Practice Mindfulness:

Mindfulness practices can help you remain grounded in the present moment. When we're present, we can better acknowledge our feelings without judgment, allowing us to explore vulnerability without fear.

1. Set Boundaries:

While vulnerability involves openness, it's also crucial to establish boundaries. Know your limits and choose the moments in which you feel comfortable sharing your true self.

1. Celebrate Small Wins:

Acknowledge the courage it takes to be vulnerable. Celebrate moments when you choose to express your feelings or share your struggles. Each step forward builds resilience.

The Strength of Community

IN OUR JOURNEYS, THE strength of a community cannot be overlooked. When we create an environment where vulnerability is honored, we lay the groundwork for collective strength. Women supporting women, sharing their stories, and fostering connection create a tapestry of resilience that uplifts everyone involved.

The beauty of a community lies in its ability to amplify individual strengths. When we share our stories, we validate one another's experiences and remind each other that we are not alone in our struggles. A woman's strength does not diminish when she shares her vulnerabilities; instead, it often inspires others to embrace their own.

AS WE CONCLUDE THIS chapter, let us carry forward the understanding that strength is not a monolith defined by external appearances. It is a dynamic interplay of emotional, mental, and spiritual elements. Embracing vulnerability is a courageous act that invites authenticity and connection.

Strength lies in the stories we tell, the connections we forge, and the resilience we cultivate together. By redefining strength to include vulnerability, we empower ourselves and each other to rise above the limitations of traditional stereotypes. Let us celebrate this transformation, knowing that within each act of vulnerability, we uncover the true essence of strength.

Chapter 2: Self-Discovery

Uncovering Your Authentic Self

The journey of self-discovery is one of the most profound and transformative experiences we can undertake. It involves peeling back the layers of societal expectations, familial roles, and self-imposed limitations to uncover the essence of who we truly are. This process is essential not only for personal growth but also for living a fulfilling life aligned with our values and passions.

Exercises to Help Identify Your True Self

Values Exploration:

Begin by listing your core values. What principles guide your decisions? Consider aspects such as honesty, creativity, compassion, or adventure. Write down the values that resonate most with you and rank them in order of importance. Reflect on how these values align with your current life and where you may need to make adjustments.

Passion Inventory:

Create a list of activities that bring you joy. Think of moments when you felt most alive—what were you doing? This could include hobbies, career aspirations, or volunteer work. Analyze your list to identify common themes, which can provide insight into your authentic self.

Strengths and Weaknesses Analysis:

Acknowledge your strengths and weaknesses by conducting a personal SWOT analysis (Strengths, Weaknesses, Opportunities, Threats). Understanding your strengths can help you leverage them in your pursuits, while recognizing your weaknesses allows for personal growth.

Visualization Exercise:

Imagine your ideal self in five years. Visualize what your life looks like, where you are, and who you are with. Write a detailed description of this vision, focusing on the feelings associated with it. This exercise can reveal aspirations and qualities you wish to embody.

Journaling for Self-Discovery:

Dedicate time each day to journaling. Pose open-ended questions such as, "What brings me joy?" or "What am I afraid of?" Allow yourself to write freely without judgment. Over time, patterns and themes will emerge, illuminating aspects of your authentic self.

The Importance of Self-Awareness in Personal Growth

SELF-AWARENESS IS THE cornerstone of personal growth. It is the ability to recognize and understand your thoughts, emotions, and behaviors, providing a clear picture of how they influence your life. Self-awareness empowers you to make conscious choices that align with your values and aspirations.

- Mindfulness Practices:

INCORPORATE MINDFULNESS techniques into your daily routine. Whether through meditation, deep breathing, or mindful walking, these practices enhance your ability to remain present and aware of your inner landscape.

- Feedback Loop:

ENGAGE WITH TRUSTED friends or mentors who can provide honest feedback about your behaviors and blind spots. Constructive criticism can be a powerful tool for growth, helping you see yourself from different perspectives.

- Reflective Questioning:

REGULARLY ASK YOURSELF reflective questions such as, "Why do I react this way in certain situations?" or "What triggers my insecurities?" This practice fosters deeper self-understanding and encourages growth.

Self-awareness allows us to identify patterns in our behavior and emotional responses, providing insight into how our past influences our present. As we become more aware of ourselves, we can take active steps to change our narratives and align our lives with our authentic selves.

Embracing Your Story: The Past as a Teacher

OUR PAST EXPERIENCES shape our identities, often serving as the foundation upon which we build our present selves. However, the stories we tell ourselves about these experiences can either empower us or hold us back. Embracing our stories involves acknowledging our past, learning from it, and reframing it positively to foster personal growth.

Analyzing Personal Narratives and Their Impact on Identity

PERSONAL NARRATIVES are the stories we tell ourselves about our experiences. These narratives shape our beliefs and self-perception, influencing how we approach life. For instance, if you view a past failure as a definitive marker of your capabilities, it can hinder your willingness to take risks in the future.

- Identify Key Experiences:

Reflect on significant events in your life that have shaped your identity. What lessons did you learn from these experiences? How have they influenced your beliefs about yourself?

- Recognize Patterns:

Analyze the themes in your narratives. Are there recurring motifs of struggle, resilience, or triumph? Recognizing these patterns helps you understand how your past has informed your present.

+

Techniques for Reframing Past Experiences Positively

The Reframing Exercise:

Choose a past experience that holds negative connotations. Write it down in detail, focusing on the emotions associated with it. Then, rewrite the narrative, emphasizing the lessons learned and the strength gained from the experience. This reframing can shift your perspective from victimhood to empowerment.

Gratitude Journaling:

Each day, write down three things you are grateful for, including aspects of your past that have contributed to your growth. This practice helps cultivate a positive outlook and acknowledges the role of past experiences in shaping your present.

Creating a Vision Board:

Use a vision board to visualize your future self. Include images, quotes, and symbols that represent your aspirations and the lessons learned from your past. This visual representation serves as a reminder of your journey and the strength you've gained.

Share Your Story:

Engage in storytelling, whether through writing, speaking, or art. Sharing your story not only reinforces your understanding of your past but also allows others to connect with your experiences. This connection fosters a sense of community and can inspire others on their journeys.

Forgiveness and Release:

Practice forgiveness, both for yourself and others. Holding onto past grievances can weigh heavily on your spirit. Write a letter expressing your feelings, even if you never send it. Acknowledge the pain, but also your desire to release it, creating space for growth.

CONCLUSION: THE PATH of Self-Discovery

The journey of self-discovery is ongoing, filled with challenges and triumphs. As we uncover our authentic selves and embrace our stories, we open ourselves to a life rich in meaning and connection. By engaging in exercises that foster self-awareness and reframing our narratives, we empower ourselves to grow and evolve.

Self-discovery is not merely about finding who we are; it is about becoming who we are meant to be. Each step on this path brings us closer to our true selves, allowing us to live authentically and embrace the beautiful complexities of our lives. As we continue this journey, let us cherish our past as a teacher, guiding us toward a future filled with possibility and strength.

Chapter 3: Building Resilience

The Science of Resilience

RESILIENCE IS THE REMARKABLE ability to adapt and thrive in the face of adversity. Psychological research has illuminated this concept, revealing that resilience is not merely a personality trait but a dynamic process that anyone can cultivate. It encompasses a range of behaviors, thoughts, and actions that enable individuals to cope with stress and rebound from challenges.

Insights into Psychological Research on Resilience

RESEARCHERS LIKE DR. Martin Seligman, a pioneer in positive psychology, have studied resilience extensively. His work demonstrates that resilient individuals share certain cognitive patterns and emotional responses that help them navigate life's difficulties. Rather than viewing setbacks as insurmountable obstacles, resilient people see them as opportunities for growth. This shift in perspective—what psychologists call a "growth mindset"—is fundamental to resilience.

Studies have shown that resilience can be cultivated through various means. For instance, social support is a critical factor. People who maintain strong relationships tend to cope better with stress and recover more quickly from setbacks. This finding underscores the importance of community and connection, reminding us that we do not have to face challenges alone.

Common Traits of Resilient Individuals

Optimism:

Resilient individuals maintain a hopeful outlook. They believe that challenges are temporary and that they can influence their outcomes through effort and perseverance.

Emotional Awareness:

They possess a keen understanding of their emotions, allowing them to process feelings rather than suppress them. This emotional intelligence enables them to navigate difficult situations more effectively.

Flexibility:

Resilient people are adaptable, able to adjust their plans and approaches in response to changing circumstances. This flexibility allows them to find alternative solutions when faced with obstacles.

Problem-Solving Skills:

They approach challenges with a solutions-oriented mindset, seeking ways to overcome difficulties rather than dwelling on the problems themselves.

Sense of Purpose:

Resilient individuals often have a clear sense of purpose, which guides them during tough times. This sense of meaning provides motivation and a reason to persevere.

UNDERSTANDING THESE traits is the first step toward building resilience within ourselves. It's essential to recognize that resilience is not about avoiding adversity; rather, it is about facing it head-on with the tools and mindset necessary to thrive.

Strategies for Bouncing Back

BUILDING RESILIENCE is a journey that requires intention and practice. Here are practical strategies to cultivate resilience in your daily life:

1. Develop a Strong Support System

SURROUND YOURSELF WITH positive, supportive individuals who uplift and encourage you. Foster relationships with friends, family, mentors, or community groups that can provide emotional and practical support. Share your challenges and successes with them; a robust support network acts as a buffer against stress and adversity.

2. Embrace a Growth Mindset

Cultivating a growth mindset means viewing challenges as opportunities for learning and growth. When you encounter setbacks, ask yourself: "What can I learn from this experience?" This mindset shift can transform failures into stepping stones toward success, allowing you to develop resilience over time.

3. Practice Self-Care

PHYSICAL WELL-BEING is intricately linked to emotional resilience. Prioritize self-care through regular exercise, nutritious meals, and sufficient sleep. Engage in activities that promote relaxation and joy, whether it's reading, painting, or spending time in nature. A healthy body supports a resilient mind.

4. Set Realistic Goals

ESTABLISHING ACHIEVABLE, short-term goals can help you regain a sense of control when life feels overwhelming. Break larger tasks into smaller, manageable steps. Celebrate each accomplishment, no matter how minor, to reinforce your ability to overcome obstacles and build momentum.

5. Cultivate Emotional Awareness

DEVELOPING EMOTIONAL awareness involves acknowledging and understanding your feelings. Keep a journal to reflect on your emotional responses to daily challenges. By identifying patterns in your emotions, you can learn to manage them more effectively and respond to stress with greater resilience.

6. Learn Problem-Solving Skills

WHEN FACED WITH CHALLENGES, adopt a proactive approach. Outline the problem, brainstorm possible solutions, and evaluate the best course of action. This structured approach not only helps in addressing the issue at hand but also builds confidence in your ability to tackle future challenges.

7. Reframe Negative Thoughts

OUR THOUGHTS SIGNIFICANTLY influence our emotional responses. When negative thoughts arise, practice reframing them. Instead of thinking, "I can't handle this," shift to, "This is challenging, but I can take it one step at a time." This shift helps in reducing anxiety and fostering a resilient mindset.

Mindset Shifts to Embrace Challenges

EMBRACING CHALLENGES requires a fundamental shift in how we perceive obstacles. Here are some mindset shifts to help you embrace adversity as an integral part of your growth journey:

From Fear to Curiosity:

Instead of fearing failure, approach it with curiosity. Ask yourself what lessons the experience has to offer. Curiosity can transform fear into an opportunity for exploration and learning.

From Perfectionism to Progress:

Shift your focus from perfection to progress. Understand that setbacks are a natural part of any journey. Celebrate the small wins and recognize that growth often occurs in the face of imperfection.

From Isolation to Connection:

Rather than withdrawing during tough times, lean into your relationships. Sharing your struggles with others can foster connection and mutual support, reinforcing your resilience.

From Fixed Mindset to Adaptive Thinking:

Challenge the belief that your abilities are static. Embrace the idea that you can learn and grow through effort and experience. This adaptive thinking fosters resilience in the face of setbacks.

Conclusion: The Power of Resilience

BUILDING RESILIENCE is a lifelong journey that empowers us to navigate the complexities of life. By understanding the science behind resilience and embracing practical strategies, we can cultivate the inner strength needed to bounce back from adversity.

Resilience is not a trait reserved for a select few; it is a skill that can be developed by anyone willing to invest in themselves. As we shift our mindsets and adopt practices that nurture resilience, we unlock our potential to thrive, regardless of the challenges we encounter.

Remember, resilience is not about avoiding hardship; it's about facing life's storms with courage, determination, and an unwavering belief in our ability to rise again. Embrace the journey, knowing that every challenge is an opportunity for growth and transformation. In the end, resilience is not just about survival; it's about flourishing in the midst of adversity.

Chapter 4: Cultivating Confidence

Overcoming Self-Doubt

Self-doubt is a universal experience that can hinder our progress and dampen our spirits. It often whispers insidiously in our minds, convincing us we aren't good enough, smart enough, or worthy enough. But acknowledging and addressing self-doubt is the first step toward cultivating lasting confidence.

Identifying Sources of Self-Doubt

SELF-DOUBT CAN ARISE from various sources, including past experiences, societal pressures, and internalized beliefs.

Past Experiences:

NEGATIVE EXPERIENCES, particularly from childhood or early adulthood, can plant seeds of doubt. A harsh critique from a teacher, a failed relationship, or missed opportunities can create lasting impressions that shape our self-perception.

Societal Pressures:

THE MEDIA OFTEN PERPETUATES unrealistic standards of success, beauty, and intelligence. When we compare ourselves to curated images of others, it can lead to feelings of inadequacy.

Internalized Beliefs:

SOMETIMES, SELF-DOUBT is rooted in deeply held beliefs about ourselves. These beliefs might stem from our upbringing, cultural context, or negative reinforcement we've received over time.

How Self-Doubt Manifests

SELF-DOUBT CAN MANIFEST in various ways, including:

Procrastination:

Doubting our abilities can lead to avoidance of tasks or opportunities, leaving us stuck and unfulfilled.

Perfectionism:

THE DESIRE TO BE PERFECT can be a mask for self-doubt, leading us to overwork or constantly critique our efforts.

Fear of Failure:

AN OVERWHELMING FEAR of failing can paralyze us, making it difficult to take risks or pursue new challenges.

Strategies for Reframing Negative Thoughts

OVERCOMING SELF-DOUBT involves recognizing and reframing the negative thoughts that plague us. Here are practical strategies to combat self-doubt and cultivate a more empowering mindset:

Identify Negative Thoughts:

Start by keeping a journal where you document moments of self-doubt. Write down the specific thoughts you have in those moments, such as "I'm not talented enough" or "I'll never succeed."

Challenge Those Thoughts:

Once you've identified negative thoughts, challenge their validity. Ask yourself: Is there concrete evidence that supports this belief? What would I tell a friend who expressed this doubt?

Reframe the Narrative:

Replace negative thoughts with positive affirmations. For example, instead of thinking, "I can't do this," reframe it to, "I am capable of learning and growing through this challenge."

Visualize Success:

Spend a few minutes each day visualizing yourself succeeding. Picture the steps you'll take and how it will feel to achieve your goals. Visualization can help shift your mindset from fear to confidence.

Practice Gratitude:

Regularly reflect on your strengths and accomplishments. Create a gratitude journal focused on what you appreciate about yourself and your journey. This practice helps to ground you in positivity.

Seek Support:

Share your feelings of self-doubt with trusted friends or mentors. They can provide perspective, encouragement, and remind you of your strengths when you struggle to see them.

Techniques to Boost Self-Esteem

BUILDING SELF-ESTEEM is a crucial component of cultivating confidence. Here are activities and affirmations to enhance your self-worth:

Activities to Enhance Self-Confidence

Set Achievable Goals:

Start small by setting realistic, achievable goals. Whether it's completing a project, trying a new hobby, or simply making your bed each morning, each accomplishment builds momentum and confidence.

Engage in Self-Care:

Taking care of your physical and mental health is vital for self-esteem. Establish a self-care routine that includes regular exercise, healthy eating, and time for relaxation. When you feel good physically, it often reflects positively on your self-image.

Step Outside Your Comfort Zone:

Challenge yourself to try new things that make you slightly uncomfortable. This could be public speaking, attending a social event, or taking a class. Each small step outside your comfort zone reinforces your ability to handle challenges.

Practice Assertiveness:

Learning to express your needs and opinions confidently is a key aspect of self-esteem. Start by practicing assertive communication in low-stakes situations, gradually building up to more significant conversations.

Celebrate Your Accomplishments:

Create a "success jar" where you write down your achievements, big or small, and place them in the jar. On tough days, read through these notes to remind yourself of your capabilities.

Affirmations to Enhance Self-Confidence

AFFIRMATIONS ARE POWERFUL tools for reshaping our beliefs about ourselves. Here are some affirmations to incorporate into your daily routine:

- "I am enough just as I am."
- "I have the strength and ability to overcome challenges."
- "I celebrate my unique qualities and embrace my journey."
- "I trust myself to make the best decisions for my life."
- "Every day, I grow stronger and more confident."

Repeat these affirmations daily, whether in the mirror, during meditation, or as part of your morning routine. Over time, affirmations can help rewire your mindset and foster a more positive self-image.

The Role of Accomplishments in Building Self-Worth

ACCOMPLISHMENTS, REGARDLESS of their size, play a crucial role in building self-esteem. Each achievement reinforces the belief that we are capable and deserving of success.

- Recognize Progress:

It's important to acknowledge progress rather than fixating solely on end results. Celebrate the effort, determination, and resilience it took to reach your goals.

- Document Your Journey:

KEEP A JOURNAL WHERE you track your accomplishments and milestones. This tangible record serves as a reminder of your growth and serves as motivation during times of self-doubt.

- Embrace Failure as Feedback:

RATHER THAN VIEWING failure as a reflection of your worth, see it as a necessary step in the journey toward success. Each setback provides valuable lessons and insights, contributing to your overall growth.

Conclusion: The Path to Lasting Confidence

CULTIVATING CONFIDENCE is an ongoing journey that involves overcoming self-doubt, enhancing self-esteem, and embracing our unique stories. By identifying the sources of our self-doubt and actively reframing negative thoughts, we empower ourselves to rise above the challenges we face.

The techniques and affirmations outlined in this chapter are not merely quick fixes; they are tools that, when practiced consistently, can lead to profound transformations in how we view ourselves and our capabilities.

Remember, confidence is not about being fearless; it's about acknowledging fear and choosing to move forward regardless. Each step you take toward building your confidence strengthens your ability to face the world with authenticity and resilience. Embrace this journey with an open heart, knowing that you are worthy of all the success and joy life has to offer.

Chapter 5: Setting Boundaries

The Importance of Healthy Boundaries

In a world that often blurs the lines between personal and professional life, the concept of boundaries can feel both foreign and essential. Boundaries are the invisible lines we draw around ourselves, defining what we are comfortable with and what we are not.

They serve as the framework for how we interact with others, protecting our mental and emotional well-being.

Understanding What Boundaries Are and Why They Matter

AT ITS CORE, A BOUNDARY is a guideline that outlines how we want to be treated by others. It encompasses our physical, emotional, and time-related limits. Healthy boundaries can be thought of as the self-care armor we wear to protect our energy and well-being. Without them, we risk becoming overwhelmed, resentful, or even burnt out.

Setting boundaries is not about building walls; it's about creating a space where we can thrive. They allow us to prioritize our needs and make choices that align with our values. Healthy boundaries foster mutual respect in relationships, encouraging open communication and understanding. When we communicate our limits clearly, we create healthier interactions and prevent misunderstandings.

The Connection Between Boundaries and Self-Respect

BOUNDARIES ARE FUNDAMENTALLY linked to self-respect. When we set and uphold boundaries, we affirm our worthiness and acknowledge our right to have our needs met. Conversely, neglecting to establish boundaries can lead to feelings of guilt, resentment, and diminished self-esteem.

Think about it: when you say "yes" to something that doesn't align with your values or depletes your energy, you're sending a message to yourself that your needs aren't important. On the other hand, when you assertively communicate your boundaries, you reinforce the idea that you deserve respect, care, and consideration.

Boundaries are not only a reflection of how we see ourselves but also how we invite others to treat us. By honoring our own limits, we inspire those around us to do the same.

Practical Tips for Assertive Communication

SETTING BOUNDARIES can feel daunting, especially if you're not used to asserting your needs. But with practice, it becomes easier. Here's a step-by-step guide to help you set and maintain boundaries effectively.

Step 1: Identify Your Limits

BEFORE YOU CAN COMMUNICATE your boundaries, you need to know what they are. Reflect on situations where you feel overwhelmed or uncomfortable. Ask yourself:

- What are the triggers that cause me stress or discomfort?
- Are there specific people or situations that frequently cross my limits?
- What do I need to feel safe and respected in my relationships?

Take some time to write down your observations. This will serve as your personal boundary blueprint.

Step 2: Communicate Clearly and Directly

WHEN IT COMES TO SETTING boundaries, clarity is key. Use "I" statements to express your needs and feelings. For example:

- Instead of saying, "You always interrupt me," try, "I feel frustrated when I'm interrupted during our conversations. I'd appreciate it if we could take turns speaking."

This approach minimizes defensiveness and fosters understanding. Be direct and concise—there's no need for long explanations or justifications.

Step 3: Practice Active Listening

SETTING BOUNDARIES isn't just about speaking your truth; it's also about listening to others. When you communicate your needs, give the other person space to respond. Listen actively and validate their feelings. This not only strengthens your relationship but also shows that you value their perspective.

Step 4: Be Prepared for Pushback

NOT EVERYONE WILL IMMEDIATELY accept your boundaries, and that's okay. Be prepared for resistance or questions. Stay calm and reiterate your needs if necessary. Remember, setting boundaries is about what feels right for you, not about pleasing others.

Step 5: Reinforce Your Boundaries

ONCE YOU'VE SET A BOUNDARY, it's essential to uphold it. If someone crosses your limit, address it promptly. Remind them of your boundary and express how their actions affect you. Consistency is key; it reinforces the importance of your needs and establishes a precedent for how you expect to be treated.

Step 6: Know When to Walk Away

SOMETIMES, DESPITE your best efforts, certain relationships may remain toxic or draining. If your boundaries are consistently disrespected, it might be time to evaluate whether that relationship serves your well-being. Remember, it's okay to prioritize your mental and emotional health.

Role-Playing Scenarios to Practice Assertiveness

ROLE-PLAYING CAN BE an effective way to build confidence in communicating your boundaries. Here are a few scenarios to practice:

Scenario 1: The Overbearing Colleague

Situation: A colleague frequently asks you to take on additional work, making you feel overwhelmed.

Response:

- YOU: "I APPRECIATE your confidence in me, but I'm currently at capacity with my workload. I won't be able to take on any more tasks at the moment. Can we discuss prioritizing what I already have?"

Scenario 2: The Friend Who Always Cancels Plans

Situation: A friend frequently cancels at the last minute, leaving you feeling unimportant.

Response:

- YOU: "I VALUE OUR time together, but when plans are canceled last minute, it makes me feel like my time isn't respected. I'd love to set a date that works for both of us and commit to it."

Scenario 3: Family Expectations

Situation: Family members often pressure you to participate in events you're not interested in.

Response:

- YOU: "I APPRECIATE the invitations, but I need to prioritize my own well-being. I'll need to decline this time. I hope you understand."

By practicing these scenarios, you'll feel more prepared to assert your boundaries in real-life situations.

Conclusion: Embracing the Power of Boundaries

Setting boundaries is a powerful act of self-love and self-respect. It's an essential skill that allows us to prioritize our needs, foster healthy relationships, and cultivate a sense of empowerment.

Remember that establishing boundaries is not selfish; it's necessary for your well-being. As you practice assertive communication, you'll find that not only do you become more confident, but your relationships will also grow stronger and more respectful.

Embrace this journey of setting boundaries, knowing that you have the right to create a life that honors your needs and aspirations. The path may feel challenging at times, but with each step, you're affirming your worth and cultivating the respect you deserve. As you establish your boundaries, you're not just protecting yourself—you're inviting a more fulfilling and authentic life into your world.

Chapter 6: Nurturing Relationships

Building a Supportive Network

Our relationships profoundly influence our well-being and personal growth. Surrounding ourselves with a supportive network can provide the encouragement and positivity we need to thrive. However, recognizing toxic relationships is equally crucial for cultivating a healthier emotional landscape.

Identifying Toxic Relationships

TOXIC RELATIONSHIPS can drain our energy and self-esteem, making it essential to identify signs of negativity. Common indicators of toxic dynamics include:

Constant Criticism: If someone consistently belittles or criticizes you, it can undermine your self-worth. Healthy relationships uplift and encourage, while toxic ones can leave you feeling inadequate.

Lack of Support: A supportive friend or partner celebrates your successes and stands by you during tough times. If someone consistently dismisses your achievements or fails to provide emotional support, it may be time to reassess the relationship.

Manipulation or Control: Toxic relationships often involve manipulation, where one person exerts control over another's thoughts or actions. This can manifest as guilt-tripping, shaming, or gaslighting.

Emotional Drain: After interacting with someone, do you feel energized or depleted? Healthy connections leave us feeling fulfilled, while toxic ones often result in emotional exhaustion.

Recognizing these patterns is the first step toward creating a more positive environment. It's okay to distance yourself from relationships that no longer serve your well-being.

The Importance of Surrounding Yourself with Positivity

Building a supportive network involves actively seeking out relationships that inspire and uplift you. Here's why positivity matters:

- Emotional Resilience: Positive relationships enhance our emotional resilience, providing a safety net during challenging times. A supportive friend can help you reframe negative situations, encouraging a more optimistic outlook.

- Growth and Development: Healthy connections foster personal growth. Engaging with individuals who challenge and motivate you can lead to new perspectives and opportunities for learning.

- Community and Belonging: Surrounding yourself with positive people cultivates a sense of belonging. Whether it's friends, family, or community members, having a support system can alleviate feelings of loneliness and isolation.

Tips for Cultivating Meaningful Connections

BE INTENTIONAL:

Reflect on the qualities you value in relationships. Seek out individuals who embody those traits—kindness, honesty, support. Intentionality in your connections helps foster meaningful bonds.

Invest Time and Effort:

Relationships require nurturing. Make an effort to spend quality time with those who uplift you. Small gestures, like checking in or sharing a meal, can strengthen your connections.

Practice Vulnerability:

Authentic connections are built on vulnerability. Share your thoughts and feelings honestly, allowing others to do the same. This openness fosters deeper understanding and trust.

ENGAGE IN ACTIVITIES Together:

Participate in activities that bring you joy. Whether it's joining a book club, taking a class, or engaging in a hobby, shared experiences create lasting memories and bonds.

Be a Source of Positivity:

Just as you seek uplifting connections, strive to be a positive influence in others' lives. Celebrate their successes, offer support during tough times, and practice kindness.

The Art of Healthy Conflict Resolution

CONFLICT IS A NATURAL part of any relationship. How we approach and resolve conflicts can significantly impact our connections. Healthy conflict resolution is about understanding, respect, and constructive dialogue.

Techniques for Addressing Conflicts Constructively

Stay Calm and Centered:

When conflicts arise, take a moment to breathe and center yourself. Approach the situation with a calm demeanor to prevent escalation.

Choose the Right Time and Place:

Timing and setting matter. Address conflicts in a private, comfortable space where both parties can speak freely without distractions.

Use "I" Statements:

Communicate your feelings and needs using "I" statements to express how the situation affects you. For example, say, "I feel hurt when plans are canceled last minute," instead of "You always cancel plans."

Focus on Solutions:

Instead of dwelling on the problem, shift the conversation toward finding solutions. Collaborate on potential resolutions that consider both perspectives. This teamwork fosters mutual respect and understanding.

Take Responsibility:

Acknowledge your role in the conflict. Taking responsibility for your actions demonstrates maturity and encourages the other person to do the same.

The Importance of Active Listening and Empathy

ACTIVE LISTENING IS a vital component of effective conflict resolution. It involves fully focusing on the speaker, understanding their message, and responding thoughtfully.

Listen Without Interrupting: Allow the other person to express their feelings without interjecting. This shows respect for their perspective and fosters open communication.

Reflect Back: After the other person shares their thoughts, reflect back what you've heard to ensure understanding. For instance, you might say, "What I'm hearing is that you feel overlooked when I don't include you in decisions."

Validate Feelings: Acknowledge the other person's feelings, even if you disagree with their perspective. Validating emotions helps to diffuse tension and shows that you care.

Practice Empathy: Put yourself in the other person's shoes. Consider their experiences and emotions. This understanding can bridge gaps and lead to more constructive conversations.

Conclusion: Nurturing Relationships for Personal Growth

NURTURING RELATIONSHIPS is a vital aspect of personal growth and well-being. By recognizing toxic dynamics and surrounding ourselves with positive influences, we create an environment that fosters support and encouragement. Healthy connections enhance our emotional resilience, allowing us to navigate life's challenges more effectively.

Equally important is the ability to address conflicts constructively. Healthy conflict resolution, grounded in active listening and empathy, strengthens relationships and fosters deeper connections.

As you embark on this journey of nurturing relationships, remember that it's a two-way street. Your efforts to cultivate meaningful connections will not only enrich your life but also inspire those around you. Embrace the beauty of relationships, knowing that each connection is an opportunity for growth, understanding, and shared joy. By nurturing positive bonds, you'll create a life filled with support, love, and connection—an essential foundation for a fulfilling journey ahead.

Chapter 7: Embracing Change

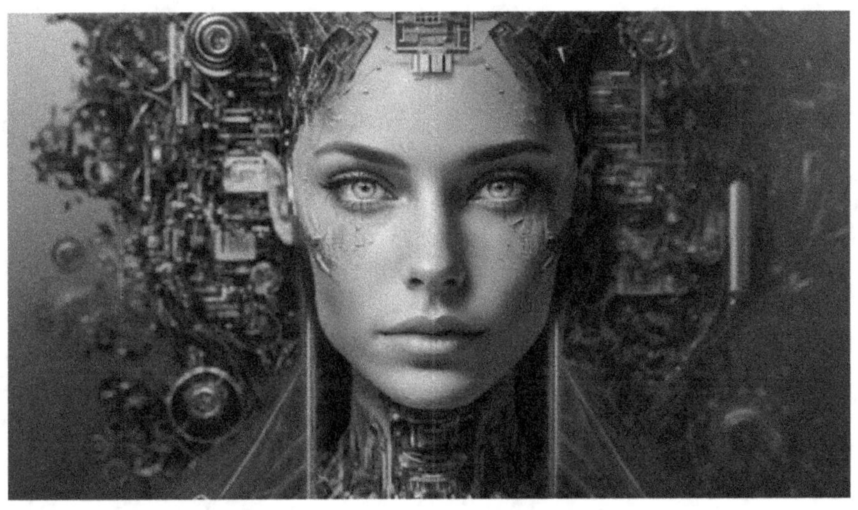

Navigating Life Transitions

Change is one of life's few constants. From moving to a new city, starting a new job, experiencing a relationship shift, or welcoming a new family member, life transitions can be both exhilarating and daunting. Each change brings its own set of emotions, challenges, and opportunities for growth.

Discussing Common Life Changes and Their Emotional Impacts

LIFE TRANSITIONS OFTEN evoke a whirlwind of feelings—excitement, anxiety, uncertainty, and sometimes even grief. Here are some common transitions and their emotional impacts:

1. Career Changes:

Whether it's starting a new job, getting a promotion, or facing job loss, career changes can trigger feelings of insecurity and fear. The unknown can be intimidating, but it also opens doors to new opportunities and personal growth.

Relationship Shifts:

Changes in relationships—be it a new romance, a breakup, or a friendship ending—can lead to feelings of loss and confusion. These shifts challenge us to reevaluate our identities and redefine what we seek in our connections.

Moving:

Relocating can bring excitement but also sadness as we leave behind familiar places and people. This change often requires us to build new support systems and adapt to different environments.

Health Changes:

Whether facing a new diagnosis or making lifestyle changes, health-related transitions can profoundly impact our emotional and physical well-being. These experiences often push us to confront our vulnerabilities and embrace resilience.

Life Milestones:

Major life events, such as becoming a parent, graduating, or retiring, can provoke mixed feelings of joy and apprehension. They often require significant adjustments and new roles that can feel overwhelming.

Tools for Adapting to New Circumstances with Grace

NAVIGATING CHANGE IS rarely straightforward, but there are tools we can use to adapt more gracefully:

Practice Self-Compassion:

Acknowledge that it's normal to feel a range of emotions during transitions. Treat yourself with the same kindness you would offer a friend. Remember, it's okay to struggle as you adjust to new circumstances.

Stay Present:

Mindfulness techniques, such as meditation or deep breathing, can help anchor you in the present moment. By focusing on what you can control right now, you can alleviate anxiety about the future.

Seek Support:

Lean on your support network. Share your feelings with friends, family, or mentors who can provide guidance and encouragement. Sometimes, simply talking about your experiences can provide clarity and comfort.

Set Small Goals:

Break down the transition into manageable steps. Whether it's learning a new skill for a job or finding new social circles after a move, setting small, achievable goals can help you feel a sense of progress and control.

Embrace Flexibility:

Be open to the idea that change may not unfold as you expected. Embracing flexibility allows you to adapt and find new paths rather than feeling trapped by rigid plans.

Reflect and Journal:

Keep a journal to process your thoughts and feelings during transitions. Reflecting on your experiences can provide insight, clarity, and a sense of empowerment as you navigate the unknown.

Turning Obstacles into Opportunities

LIFE'S CHALLENGES CAN often feel like insurmountable obstacles. However, many inspiring women have transformed these challenges into profound opportunities for growth and self-discovery.

Inspiring Stories of Women Who Have Transformed Challenges into Growth

From Loss to Purpose:

Sarah lost her mother unexpectedly and found herself overwhelmed by grief. Instead of succumbing to despair, she decided to honor her mother's legacy by starting a nonprofit organization focused on mental health awareness. Through her work, Sarah found a renewed sense of purpose and community, turning her pain into a powerful catalyst for change.

Reinventing After Job Loss:

When Maria faced unexpected job loss during an economic downturn, she initially felt defeated. However, after reflecting on her passions, she decided to pursue her dream of starting a bakery. With perseverance and creativity, Maria not only launched her business but also created a space for others to gather and celebrate community, transforming a setback into a fulfilling new chapter.

Overcoming Health Challenges:

After being diagnosed with a chronic illness, Jessica felt her world was collapsing. Yet, through determination and resilience, she began advocating for others facing similar challenges. She launched a blog to share her journey, connecting with others and building a supportive community. Jessica turned her struggle into a source of strength and empowerment, inspiring countless others.

Action Steps for Shifting Perspective on Difficulties

Reframe Your Mindset:

Shift your perspective by viewing challenges as opportunities for growth. Instead of asking, "Why is this happening to me?" consider, "What can I learn from this experience?" This simple shift can open your mind to possibilities you may not have previously seen.

Create a Vision Board:

Visualize the opportunities that can arise from your challenges. A vision board filled with images and words that inspire you can serve as a powerful reminder of your goals and aspirations, helping you stay focused on the positive potential of change.

Embrace a Growth Mindset:

Adopting a growth mindset means believing that abilities and intelligence can be developed through effort and learning. Embrace the idea that setbacks are part of the journey and that each experience contributes to your personal development.

Take Action:

Identify one small step you can take toward transforming your challenge into an opportunity. Whether it's networking for a new job, enrolling in a class, or reaching out to someone for support, taking action empowers you and reinforces your agency in difficult situations.

Celebrate Your Progress:

Acknowledge and celebrate each step forward, no matter how small. By recognizing your progress, you cultivate resilience and remind yourself of your ability to navigate change.

Conclusion: Embracing Change as a Catalyst for Growth

CHANGE IS AN INEVITABLE part of life, often accompanied by challenges that test our resilience. However, by embracing change and cultivating a mindset open to growth, we can transform obstacles into opportunities for self-discovery and empowerment.

Navigating life transitions requires patience, self-compassion, and a willingness to adapt. As you encounter changes in your life, remember that you have the tools and support to navigate these shifts with grace. Each challenge can become a stepping stone toward personal growth and fulfillment.

As you embrace change, allow yourself to reflect on the inspiring stories of women who have turned their challenges into triumphs. Let their journeys remind you that obstacles can be powerful catalysts for transformation. Embrace your own path with courage and optimism, knowing that every change holds the potential for new beginnings and enriching experiences. In the end, life's changes are not just challenges to be faced—they are opportunities to flourish and become the best version of yourself.

Chapter 8: Personal Growth

The Role of Lifelong Learning

PERSONAL GROWTH IS a journey that never truly ends. One of the most powerful tools for fostering this growth is lifelong learning. Embracing a mindset of continuous education and self-improvement can profoundly impact our lives, shaping not just our skills but also our perspectives and relationships.

The Importance of Continual Learning and Self-improvement

IN A RAPIDLY CHANGING world, the ability to learn and adapt is crucial. Here are several reasons why lifelong learning is so vital:

Adaptability:

The world is constantly evolving, and the skills that were once valuable can become obsolete. Lifelong learning helps you stay relevant in your career and personal life, enabling you to adapt to new challenges with confidence.

Personal Fulfillment:

Engaging in learning experiences can provide a deep sense of fulfillment. Exploring new interests, diving into subjects you're passionate about, or picking up a new hobby can invigorate your spirit and enrich your life.

Boosting Confidence:

As you acquire new knowledge and skills, you naturally build confidence in your abilities. This newfound confidence can propel you to take on new challenges, both personally and professionally.

Broadened Perspectives:

Learning exposes you to diverse viewpoints and cultures. This broadened perspective can foster empathy and understanding, enhancing your relationships and interactions with others.

Mental Well-Being:

Engaging in learning activities can stimulate your brain, keeping it healthy and sharp. This mental engagement can contribute to overall well-being, reducing stress and promoting positive mental health.

Resources for Exploring New Skills and Knowledge

THE BEAUTY OF LIFELONG learning is that it can take many forms, and countless resources are available to help you embark on this journey:

Online Courses:

Platforms like Coursera, Udemy, and Khan Academy offer courses on virtually any topic. Whether you want to learn a new language, delve into data science, or explore creative writing, there's something for everyone.

Podcasts and Audiobooks:

For those on the go, podcasts and audiobooks are fantastic ways to absorb new information. From personal development to history, there's a wealth of knowledge available to inspire and educate.

Local Workshops and Classes:

Check your community for workshops or classes that pique your interest. Whether it's cooking, painting, or coding, hands-on experiences can deepen your learning and connect you with like-minded individuals.

Book Clubs:

Join or form a book club focused on personal development or other genres that interest you. Discussing ideas with others can enhance understanding and provide fresh insights.

Mentorship:

Seek out mentors who can provide guidance and support in your learning journey. Whether they're colleagues, friends, or professionals in your field, their insights can be invaluable.

Setting and Achieving Goals

GOAL SETTING IS A CORNERSTONE of personal growth. It provides direction, motivation, and a roadmap for achieving your dreams.

Goal-Setting Frameworks

ONE OF THE MOST EFFECTIVE frameworks for setting goals is the SMART criteria, which stands for Specific, Measurable, Achievable, Relevant, and Time-bound. Let's break it down:

Specific:

Your goal should be clear and specific. Instead of saying, "I want to get fit," try "I want to run a 5K in three months." This clarity provides a focused target.

Measurable:

Establish criteria to measure your progress. For example, track your running distance each week, so you can see your improvement over time.

Achievable:

Set realistic goals that are attainable within your current circumstances. Challenging yourself is essential, but ensure your goal is grounded in reality.

Relevant:

Your goal should align with your values and long-term objectives. Ask yourself if this goal matters to you and contributes to your overall growth.

Time-bound:

Set a deadline for your goal. This creates urgency and encourages you to take consistent action. Instead of "I want to learn Spanish," specify "I want to complete a Spanish course by the end of six months."

Strategies for Maintaining Motivation and Accountability

SETTING GOALS IS JUST the beginning; staying motivated and accountable is crucial for success. Here are some strategies to help you maintain focus:

Break It Down:

Divide your larger goal into smaller, manageable tasks. This makes it less overwhelming and provides a sense of accomplishment as you complete each step.

Create a Vision Board:

Visualize your goals by creating a vision board filled with images and words that represent what you want to achieve. Place it somewhere visible to remind you of your aspirations daily.

Develop a Routine:

Establish a consistent routine that incorporates time for working on your goals. Whether it's dedicating a specific hour each week to learning or exercise, consistency breeds progress.

Find an Accountability Partner:

Share your goals with a friend or mentor who can help keep you accountable. Regular check-ins can provide encouragement, motivation, and a sense of camaraderie.

Celebrate Milestones:

Acknowledge and celebrate your progress along the way. Recognizing small achievements boosts motivation and reinforces your commitment to your goals.

Reflect and Adjust:

Periodically review your goals and progress. Reflect on what's working and what needs adjustment. Flexibility allows you to adapt to changing circumstances while staying aligned with your aspirations.

Conclusion: The Journey of Personal Growth

PERSONAL GROWTH IS a lifelong journey, enriched by continual learning and purposeful goal-setting. Embracing this journey empowers you to navigate challenges, discover new passions, and evolve into the best version of yourself.

As you explore new skills and knowledge, remember that every step you take contributes to your personal development. Surround yourself with resources that inspire and challenge you, and never hesitate to seek support from others along the way.

Setting and achieving goals provides a framework for your growth. Use the SMART criteria to guide your goal-setting process and implement strategies that foster motivation and accountability. By breaking down your aspirations and celebrating your progress, you'll cultivate resilience and drive in the face of challenges.

Embrace the beauty of personal growth, knowing that every experience, every lesson, and every goal achieved brings you closer to realizing your full potential. The journey may be winding, but it's filled with opportunities for joy, discovery, and self-improvement. As you nurture your growth, you not only enhance your own life but also inspire those around you to embark on their own journeys of lifelong learning and transformation.

Chapter 9: Mindfulness and Well-Being

The Power of Mindfulness Practices

IN OUR FAST-PACED, often chaotic lives, mindfulness offers a sanctuary—a way to pause, breathe, and reconnect with ourselves. At its core, mindfulness is the practice of being fully present in the moment, aware of our thoughts, feelings, and surroundings without judgment. This simple yet profound shift in focus can transform how we experience life.

An Introduction to Mindfulness and Its Benefits

Mindfulness isn't just a buzzword;

IT'S A POWERFUL TOOL for improving our mental, emotional, and physical well-being. Here are some key benefits:

Reduced Stress:

Regular mindfulness practice has been shown to lower stress levels by helping us respond to challenges with greater calm. By focusing on the present, we can break the cycle of anxiety about the future or regrets about the past.

Enhanced Emotional Regulation:

Mindfulness allows us to observe our emotions without being overwhelmed by them. This awareness helps us manage our reactions, leading to healthier interactions and better relationships.

Improved Focus and Clarity:

Practicing mindfulness enhances our ability to concentrate and make decisions. By training our minds to focus on the present, we can cut through distractions and enhance our productivity.

Greater Self-Awareness:

Mindfulness fosters a deeper understanding of ourselves, our habits, and our thought patterns. This self-awareness can empower us to make intentional choices that align with our values and goals.

Increased Resilience:

Life is full of ups and downs. Mindfulness equips us with the tools to navigate these fluctuations with grace, helping us bounce back from setbacks and adapt to change more effectively.

Simple Mindfulness Exercises for Daily Life

INCORPORATING MINDFULNESS into your daily routine doesn't require hours of spare time. Here are some simple exercises you can practice anytime, anywhere:

Mindful Breathing:

Take a few moments to focus solely on your breath. Inhale deeply through your nose, hold for a moment, and exhale slowly through your mouth. As thoughts arise, gently bring your focus back to your breath. Even a few minutes of this practice can ground you.

Body Scan:

Find a comfortable position and close your eyes. Starting from the top of your head, slowly bring your attention to each part of your body, noticing any tension or sensations. This exercise helps you connect with your body and release stress.

Mindful Walking:

During a short walk, pay attention to the sensations in your feet as they touch the ground, the rhythm of your breath, and the sights and sounds around you. This practice encourages you to be present in the moment while enjoying nature.

Gratitude Journaling:

Spend a few minutes each day writing down three things you are grateful for. This practice shifts your focus from what's lacking to what's abundant in your life, fostering a positive mindset.

Mindful Eating:

Take time to savor your meals. Notice the colors, textures, and flavors of your food. Eating mindfully can enhance your appreciation for nourishment and promote healthier eating habits.

BY INTEGRATING THESE practices into your daily life, you can cultivate mindfulness and enhance your overall well-being.

Creating a Self-Care Routine

SELF-CARE IS MORE THAN just a trend; it's an essential aspect of maintaining our physical, mental, and emotional health. In a world that often prioritizes productivity over personal well-being, carving out time for self-care is crucial for long-term vitality.

Understanding the Importance of Self-Care for Well-Being

Prevention of Burnout:

Regular self-care helps prevent feelings of overwhelm and burnout. When we prioritize our well-being, we can recharge and return to our responsibilities with renewed energy.

Improved Mood:

Engaging in activities that bring us joy can boost our mood and enhance our outlook on life. Simple pleasures—like reading, gardening, or spending time with loved ones—can uplift our spirits.

Enhanced Health:

Self-care often translates to healthier choices, such as regular exercise, balanced nutrition, and sufficient sleep. Prioritizing our physical health creates a strong foundation for overall well-being.

Greater Resilience:

When we practice self-care, we build resilience against stressors. By nurturing ourselves, we develop a stronger sense of self-worth and the ability to cope with life's challenges.

A Guide to Crafting a Personalized Self-Care Plan

CREATING A SELF-CARE routine that resonates with you involves reflection and intentionality. Here's a step-by-step guide to help you craft your personalized self-care plan:

1. Reflect on Your Needs:

Take some time to assess your physical, emotional, and mental well-being. What areas feel depleted? Are there specific activities or practices that rejuvenate you?

1. Identify Self-Care Activities:

List activities that nourish your soul. This could include exercise, hobbies, meditation, time with friends, or simply enjoying a quiet moment. Choose activities that resonate with you and align with your interests.

1. Set Realistic Goals:

Aim for consistency rather than perfection. Start small—perhaps commit to a 10-minute daily walk or scheduling one self-care activity each week. Gradually increase your commitment as you feel comfortable.

1. Create a Schedule:

Incorporate self-care into your calendar. Treat it like any other important appointment. Whether it's a weekend retreat or a daily morning routine, block out time for your self-care activities.

1. Listen to Your Body and Mind:

Be attuned to your feelings. If you're feeling drained, allow yourself extra rest. If you're craving connection, reach out to a friend. Self-care is about honoring your needs in the moment.

1. Practice Boundaries:

Learn to say no to activities that drain you or commitments that overwhelm you. Prioritizing your well-being means setting boundaries that protect your energy and time.

1. Revisit and Adjust:

Life changes, and so do our needs. Periodically revisit your self-care plan and make adjustments as necessary. Celebrate the activities that uplift you and let go of those that no longer serve you.

Conclusion: Embracing Mindfulness and Self-Care

Mindfulness and self-care are powerful allies on the journey to personal growth and well-being. By embracing mindfulness practices, you can cultivate a deeper awareness of yourself and your surroundings, enhancing your ability to navigate life's challenges with grace.

Similarly, crafting a personalized self-care routine empowers you to prioritize your needs and nurture your well-being. In a world that often demands more than it gives, carving out time for yourself is a radical act of self-love.

As you incorporate mindfulness and self-care into your life, remember that this journey is deeply personal. It's about discovering what nourishes your soul and what practices resonate with you. Embrace the process with an open heart, and let each moment of mindfulness and self-care become a stepping stone toward a more fulfilling and balanced life.

By nurturing your well-being, you not only enhance your own life but also inspire those around you to prioritize their health and happiness. Together, we can create a culture that values mindfulness, self-care, and the collective journey of personal growth.

Chapter 10: Finding Your Voice Empowering Yourself Through Expression

Finding your voice is a transformative journey—one that can empower you to connect with yourself and others more deeply. Whether through writing, art, or speaking, self-expression allows you to share your unique perspective with the world. It's a powerful tool for personal growth and a means to inspire others.

Exploring Various Forms of Self-Expression

Writing:

Writing can take many forms, from journaling and poetry to blogging and storytelling. It serves as a cathartic outlet for emotions and ideas. When you put pen to paper, you not only clarify your thoughts but also give yourself permission to explore your innermost feelings. For many women, writing has become a sanctuary—an intimate space where they can articulate their experiences and aspirations.

Art:

Art transcends words. Whether you paint, draw, sculpt, or engage in crafts, artistic expression allows you to convey your feelings and thoughts in a visual language. Art can be particularly therapeutic, as it enables you to channel emotions that may be difficult to express verbally. Engaging in creative activities can also serve as a form of meditation, helping to ground you in the present moment.

Speaking:

Public speaking or sharing your voice in community forums can be empowering. It provides an opportunity to express your beliefs and advocate for what matters to you. Whether you're addressing a room full of people or sharing your story in a smaller group, speaking out can build confidence and foster connections with others who resonate with your message.

Movement:

Dance, yoga, or other forms of physical expression allow you to connect with your body and emotions. Movement is a beautiful way to express yourself without the confines of language. It can bring joy, release tension, and enhance your sense of self.

The Therapeutic Benefits of Sharing Your Voice

WHEN YOU SHARE YOUR voice, you embark on a healing journey. Here's how expressing yourself can be therapeutic:

Validation of Emotions:

Sharing your thoughts and feelings allows you to validate your experiences. When you express yourself, you acknowledge your emotions, which can lead to a deeper understanding of your own needs and desires.

Connection with Others:

By sharing your story, you create connections with those who may have experienced similar struggles. This sense of community can be profoundly comforting and reassuring. Remember, your voice can resonate with others, reminding them they are not alone.

Empowerment:

Taking the step to share your voice is an act of empowerment. You assert your right to be heard and take ownership of your narrative. This act of courage can inspire others to find and share their voices.

Clarity and Insight:

The act of articulating your thoughts can bring clarity to your emotions and experiences. Writing or speaking about your feelings can help you process complex situations and gain valuable insights.

Catalyst for Change:

Your voice can be a powerful tool for change—not only for yourself but for your community and the world. When you share your experiences and insights, you contribute to a larger narrative that can inspire action and social change.

The Importance of Advocacy and Activism

AS WOMEN, WE HAVE THE incredible potential to be agents of change. Advocacy and activism allow us to use our voices to create a better world. Every day, women across the globe are making their mark through passionate activism, advocating for equality, justice, and social change.

Discussing the Role of Women in Social Change

WOMEN HAVE ALWAYS PLAYED a vital role in social movements. From suffragettes fighting for voting rights to contemporary activists advocating for climate justice, women's voices have been instrumental in driving progress. Here are a few key points to consider:

1. Historical Legacy:

Reflect on the powerful women throughout history who have used their voices to ignite change. Their courage and resilience serve as a reminder of what's possible when we stand up for our beliefs.

2. Diverse Perspectives:

Women bring unique perspectives to social issues, often grounded in their lived experiences. This diversity of thought enriches conversations and helps address the multifaceted challenges our society faces.

3. Community Building:

Women often excel at building networks and communities. By coming together, we can amplify our voices, support one another, and create a stronger impact. Collective action is powerful.

Mentorship and Support:

As women advocate for change, we also have the opportunity to uplift and mentor others. Sharing our experiences and guiding younger generations can create a ripple effect of empowerment.

ENCOURAGING READERS to Engage in Causes They Are Passionate About

Finding your voice isn't just about self-expression; it's also about channeling that expression into action. Here are some ways to engage with causes you're passionate about:

1. Identify Your Passion:

Take time to reflect on the issues that resonate with you. What causes ignite your passion? Whether it's environmental justice, women's rights, mental health awareness, or education, identifying your passion is the first step toward meaningful engagement.

Educate Yourself: Knowledge is power.

Take the time to learn about the causes you care about. Read articles, attend workshops, or follow organizations that align with your interests. Understanding the nuances of an issue equips you to advocate effectively.

Get Involved:

Find organizations, local groups, or initiatives that align with your values. Volunteer your time, attend meetings, or participate in campaigns. Every little bit counts, and your contributions can make a real difference.

Use Your Voice:

Whether through social media, writing articles, or speaking at events, share your perspective on the issues that matter to you. Your voice can inspire others to take action and raise awareness about important causes.

Advocate for Change:

Don't be afraid to reach out to policymakers or engage in advocacy efforts. Whether it's signing petitions, attending rallies, or contacting your representatives, every action contributes to creating change.

Celebrate Small Wins:

Activism can feel overwhelming, but celebrating small victories can keep you motivated. Acknowledge progress, no matter how minor, and remind yourself that every step forward is a step in the right direction.

Conclusion: Embracing Your Voice for Change

FINDING YOUR VOICE is a profound journey of self-discovery and empowerment. Through self-expression, you can articulate your experiences, foster connections, and inspire others. As you embrace your voice, remember that you have the power to effect change—not only in your life but in the lives of others.

By engaging in advocacy and activism, you become part of a larger movement toward social change. Every woman's voice matters, and together, we can create a chorus of strength and resilience. So, share your story, advocate for what you believe in, and let your voice resonate in the world.

As you continue on your journey, know that you are not alone. Countless women stand alongside you, ready to uplift and support one another. Together, let us celebrate our voices, champion our causes, and inspire the world through the power of self-expression and action. Embrace your voice—it is a gift that can change lives.

Chapter 11: Creating a Legacy

Defining Your Vision for the Future

Creating a legacy begins with envisioning the future you want to manifest. This is not merely about what you leave behind; it's about the impact you make while you're here. By defining your vision, you set the course for your life and influence those around you.

Exercises to Help Readers Envision Their Future Selves

Visualization Exercise:

Find a quiet space where you can reflect. Close your eyes and imagine your life five, ten, or even twenty years from now. What do you see? Picture your ideal environment—where are you living, who are you with, and what are you doing? Allow yourself to immerse in this vision. Afterward, jot down your thoughts and feelings. This exercise helps clarify your desires and aspirations.

Future Self Letter:

Write a letter to your future self. Describe your achievements, experiences, and the person you have become. What lessons have you learned? What challenges have you overcome? This letter serves as a reminder of your potential and encourages you to take steps toward realizing your dreams.

Vision Board Creation:

Gather images, quotes, and symbols that resonate with your goals and dreams. Create a vision board that visually represents your aspirations. Hang it in a place where you'll see it daily, serving as a constant reminder of the future you want to create.

The Legacy Statement:

Reflect on the values and principles that are important to you. Write a short statement summarizing what you want your legacy to be. Consider what you want people to remember about you and the impact you hope to have on others. This can guide your actions and decisions moving forward.

Setting Short-Term Goals:

Once you have a vision for your future, break it down into actionable short-term goals. Identify steps you can take in the coming weeks or months that align with your long-term aspirations. Writing these down can provide a roadmap to your vision.

The Significance of Having a Personal Mission Statement

A PERSONAL MISSION statement serves as your guiding compass. It articulates your purpose, values, and vision for your life, providing clarity and direction. Here's how to craft a mission statement that resonates with you:

Identify Core Values:

Reflect on what truly matters to you. Is it family, creativity, community service, or personal growth? List your top values and consider how they influence your decisions and actions.

Define Your Purpose:

Think about your passions and strengths. What do you feel called to do? How do you want to contribute to the world? Your mission should reflect your desire to make a difference in your own unique way.

Write It Down:

Combine your core values and purpose into a concise statement. For example, "My mission is to empower women through education and creativity, fostering a community of support and growth." Keep this statement visible as a reminder of your guiding principles.

Review and Revise:

Your mission statement can evolve over time. Regularly revisit and revise it to ensure it continues to reflect your growth and aspirations.

Inspiring Others: The Ripple Effect

AS YOU CREATE A LEGACY, remember that your journey of personal growth can inspire and uplift those around you. The impact of your actions can create a ripple effect, encouraging others to pursue their dreams and strive for their own personal growth.

How Personal Growth Can Inspire and Uplift Others

Leading by Example:

When you embrace your journey of self-improvement, you naturally inspire others. Your commitment to personal growth encourages those around you to reflect on their own lives and seek positive changes.

Sharing Your Story:

Your experiences—both triumphs and challenges—can resonate deeply with others. By sharing your story, you create a connection that allows others to feel seen and understood. This vulnerability fosters a sense of community and support.

CELEBRATING SUCCESSES:

Acknowledge and celebrate your milestones, no matter how small. When you share your successes, it reminds others that growth is possible and achievable. Your triumphs can serve as motivation for someone else to pursue their own goals.

Creating Safe Spaces:

Foster an environment where others feel safe to express themselves and explore their own growth. This can be through support groups, workshops, or simply by being a compassionate friend. Your presence can empower others to share their journeys and aspirations.

Encouraging Collective Growth:

Personal growth can be contagious. When you prioritize your development, it encourages your friends, family, and colleagues to do the same. By uplifting one another, you create a community dedicated to mutual growth and support.

Ways to Mentor and Support Other Women on Their Journeys

Offer Guidance:

Share your knowledge and experiences with others. Whether through formal mentorship or casual conversations, your insights can help others navigate their paths more effectively.

Be a Listening Ear:

Sometimes, all someone needs is a supportive presence. Be there to listen to their dreams and concerns without judgment. Your empathy can provide comfort and encouragement.

Facilitate Connections:

Introduce women to others in your network who can offer support or guidance. Building connections can help amplify their opportunities and provide valuable resources.

Create Learning Opportunities:

Organize workshops, book clubs, or discussion groups focused on personal growth topics. Providing a platform for shared learning fosters a sense of community and collaboration.

Encourage Action:

Help others set and achieve their goals by holding them accountable. Celebrate their successes along the way, and encourage them to take risks and step outside their comfort zones.

Be an Advocate:

Stand up for women's rights and support causes that uplift women. Your activism can inspire others to become advocates for themselves and their communities.

Conclusion: Creating a Lasting Legacy

CREATING A LEGACY IS about more than what you leave behind; it's about how you choose to live your life and impact others. By defining your vision for the future, crafting a personal mission statement, and inspiring those around you, you build a foundation for a meaningful legacy.

As you embark on this journey, remember that your growth and achievements have the power to inspire a ripple effect. Embrace the opportunity to mentor and support other women, fostering a community where everyone can thrive.

Your legacy will be defined not only by your accomplishments but by the lives you touch and the inspiration you offer. Embrace your voice, take action, and create a legacy that reflects your values, passions, and commitment to uplifting others.

Together, let's build a future filled with hope, empowerment, and the promise of a brighter tomorrow. Your journey matters—now and always.

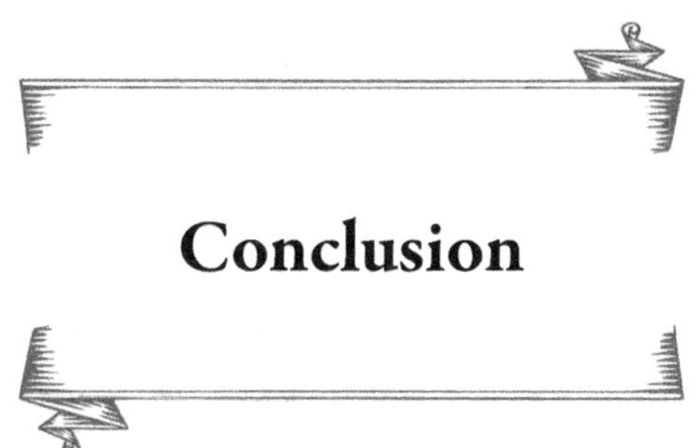

Conclusion

Embracing Your Phoenix Journey

As we reach the final pages of this book, it's essential to take a moment to reflect on the profound transformation you've embarked upon. Throughout our journey together, we have navigated the complexities of womanhood, delving deep into the experiences that shape us. Each chapter has illuminated the unique challenges and triumphs that define our paths, revealing the strength and resilience that lie within us all.

Like the mythical phoenix, which rises from its ashes renewed and revitalized, you too have the power to rise above the difficulties life presents. Your journey has not only been about overcoming obstacles but also about embracing your authentic self. Remember, transformation is not a destination but a continuous process. Each experience, whether joyous or challenging, contributes to your growth. The insights you've gained and the strength you've discovered will be invaluable as you continue to evolve.

Let this moment serve as a reminder of the incredible journey you've undertaken. Celebrate the courage it takes to confront fears, challenge societal norms, and carve your own path. You've learned that setbacks can serve as stepping stones, and that vulnerability is not a weakness but a source of strength. Embrace your journey as a testament to your resilience, and carry that spirit forward into the world.

Continuing the Transformation

AS YOU STEP BEYOND the pages of this book, it's vital to consider how you can sustain the progress you've made. Change is a lifelong commitment, and the tools you've gathered will serve as your guiding light. Here are some practical tips to help you continue your transformation and embrace a life of growth and empowerment:

Set Intentional Goals:

Take the time to set clear, meaningful goals that resonate with your values and aspirations. These goals should be specific, measurable, and achievable. Write them down and revisit them regularly to keep yourself motivated and accountable. Goals not only provide direction but also create a sense of purpose in your daily life.

Cultivate a Supportive Community:

Surround yourself with individuals who uplift and inspire you. Building a community of like-minded women fosters a sense of belonging and support. Engage in conversations, share experiences, and lean on one another for encouragement. Remember, you are not alone on this journey; together, you can uplift each other and celebrate your collective achievements.

Practice Self-Reflection:

Make self-reflection a regular practice. Set aside time to journal or meditate, allowing yourself to process your thoughts and feelings. This practice can help you gain clarity, recognize patterns, and celebrate your progress.

Reflecting on your journey will deepen your understanding of yourself and reinforce your commitment to growth.

Embrace Flexibility:

Life is full of unexpected twists and turns. Embrace flexibility and adaptability in your plans. Change is an inherent part of the journey, and being open to new experiences will enhance your resilience. When faced with challenges, remind yourself that each obstacle can lead to new opportunities for growth.

Celebrate Small Wins:

In the hustle of daily life, it's easy to overlook the small victories. Take time to celebrate your achievements, no matter how minor they may seem. Acknowledging these moments reinforces your progress and boosts your confidence. Whether it's completing a project, stepping out of your comfort zone, or simply having a good day, each win is worth celebrating.

Stay Curious:

Nurture your curiosity by seeking out new experiences and knowledge. Read books, attend workshops, and engage in activities that challenge you. Curiosity fuels growth and opens doors to new possibilities. Embrace lifelong learning as a way to continuously evolve and enrich your life.

Prioritize Self-Care:

Remember that self-care is not a luxury; it's a necessity. Make time for activities that nourish your mind, body, and soul. Whether it's spending time in nature, practicing yoga, or indulging in a creative hobby, prioritize what brings you joy and rejuvenation. A healthy balance is essential for sustaining your energy and enthusiasm on your journey.

Share Your Story:

Your experiences are powerful and can inspire others. Consider sharing your story—whether through writing, speaking, or simply having conversations. Your journey can be a source of encouragement for those facing similar struggles. By being open and vulnerable, you contribute to a culture of empowerment and support.

Moving Forward with Confidence

AS YOU MOVE FORWARD, carry the lessons you've learned with you. The journey of transformation is not always easy, but it is incredibly rewarding. Each step you take is a testament to your strength and resilience. Embrace the uncertainties of life with confidence, knowing that you have the tools to navigate whatever comes your way.

You are a force of nature, capable of creating change not just in your own life but in the lives of those around you. Your journey as a woman is filled with infinite possibilities. Stand tall, honor your journey, and embrace the path ahead. Remember, the phoenix rises not only to soar alone but to inspire others to find their wings as well.

In closing, let this book serve as a reminder of your incredible potential. Embrace the spirit of the phoenix, and let your journey of growth and resilience continue. The world awaits your brilliance—go forth and shine!

Thank you for reading

Edition 2 might me coming soon....